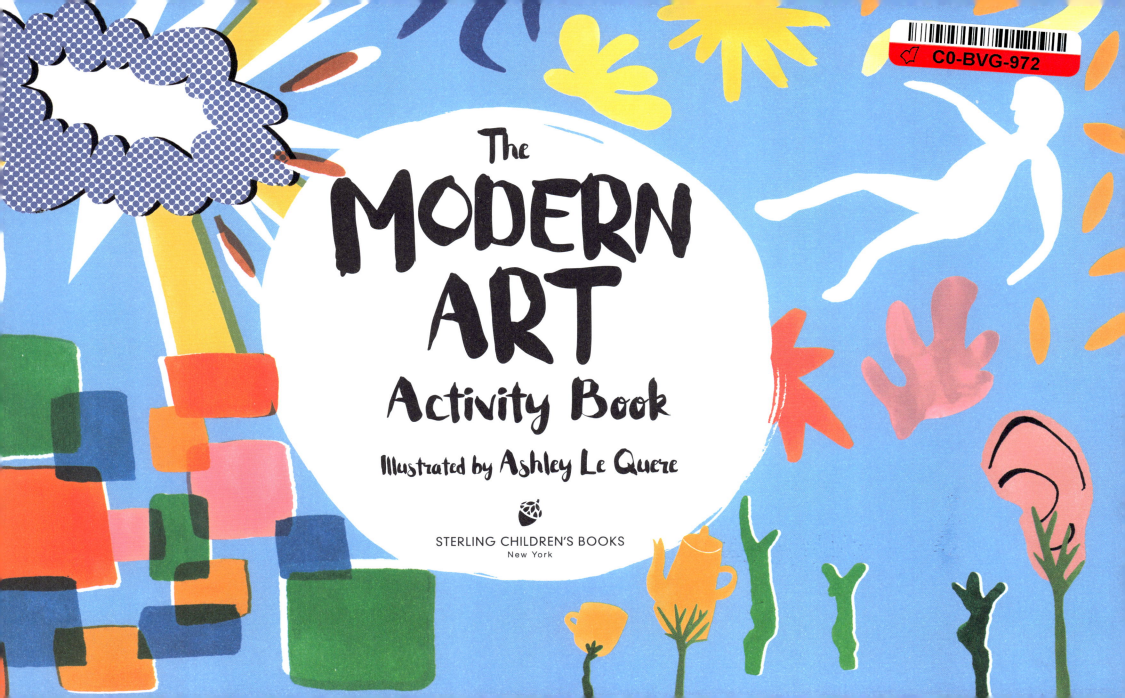

The
MODERN ART
Activity Book

Illustrated by Ashley Le Quere

STERLING CHILDREN'S BOOKS
New York

Introduction

Welcome to *The Modern Art Activity Book*. This is your own space to draw, color, and create like a modern artist. The book takes you through most of the major movements in modern art. What is a "movement"? In art, a movement is a style used by a group of artists that agree on the way in which they want to express themselves.

Get ready to travel through time to meet some of these artists and complete activities that let you re-create their unique styles. You can imitate an Impressionist, color like a Cubist, and paint like an Abstract Expressionist. There really is no better way to discover what kind of artist you are than by trying out the techniques for yourself.

As you go through the book, use the foldout timeline at the back to discover when each movement was popular.

Impressionism

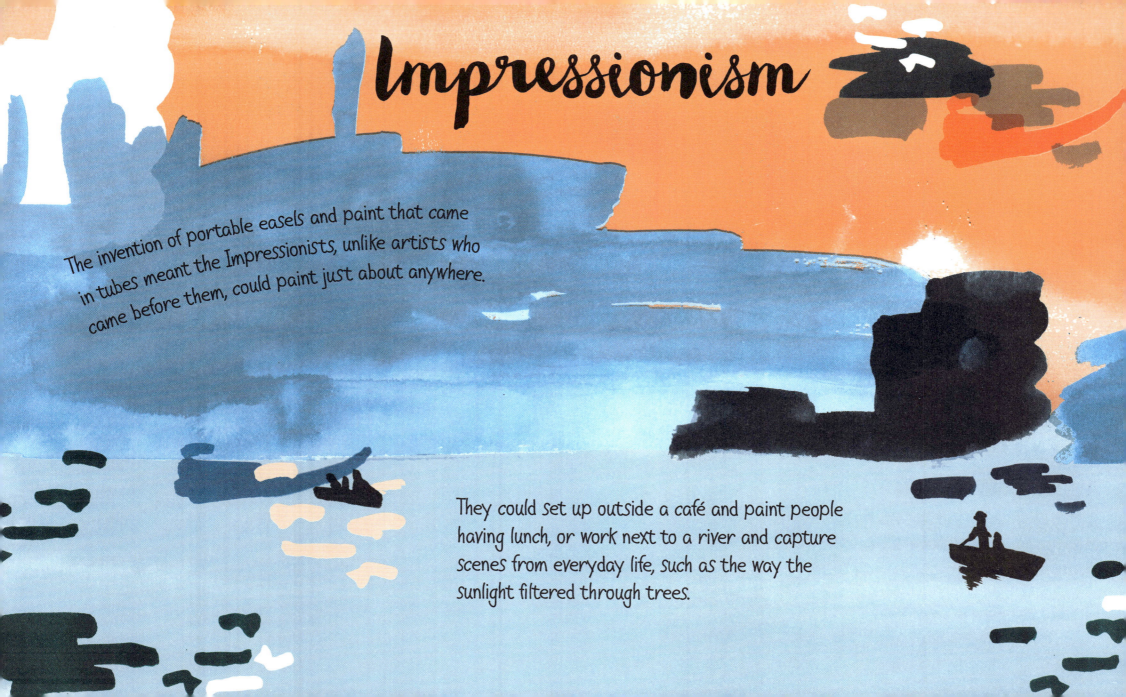

The invention of portable easels and paint that came in tubes meant the Impressionists, unlike artists who came before them, could paint just about anywhere.

They could set up outside a café and paint people having lunch, or work next to a river and capture scenes from everyday life, such as the way the sunlight filtered through trees.

Not only did the Impressionists change **where** they painted, they also changed **how** they painted. Unlike artists working in studios, they needed to work fast. Instead of trying to capture every detail of a scene, they would instead capture an "impression" of it.

Claude Monet used blobs of paint to give the "impression" of light flitting across the surface of the lily pond in his garden.

Take this book outside and draw or paint a picture as quickly as you can to capture your first **impression** of the scene around you.

Fauvism

How do the colors and shapes on this page make you feel? This would have mattered to Fauvists. Fauvists wanted to show how they felt about a subject with their art, rather than re-create exactly how it looked. They used bright colors, simple shapes, and quick brushstrokes to express their emotions.

The rough work and bold, unrealistic colors caused one French critic to call artists, such as Henri Matisse, "Les Fauves," which means "the wild beasts."

Unleash your inner "wild beast" on the next page and use your **BOLDEST COLORS** to finish the picture in the style of Les Fauves.

Cubism

Cubists didn't want to paint things exactly as they saw them. They broke down what they saw into geometric shapes and then put them back together again on the canvas.

This meant they could paint from multiple viewpoints, showing the front as well as the back and sides of an object in the same painting.

When critics first saw paintings by artists such as Georges Braque and Pablo Picasso, they thought they looked like a jumble of little cubes, so the style was called "Cubism."

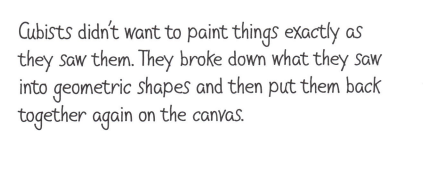

Here are some examples of Cubist images. Can you use a Cubist style to draw the objects on the opposite page?

Try to combine different views of the object in each picture.

A guitar

A person

An elephant

Your face

ORPHISM

Orphism was a movement developed by Sonia and Robert Delaunay.

They were called Orphists after the mythical musician Orpheus, whose music was said to be so beautiful it could make people, animals, and even trees follow him.

Orphists wanted to create artwork in the same way a musician composes a piece of music. They believed they could use colors and shapes in **HARMONY** with one another to describe the world around them, as a composer uses instruments and voices.

Take inspiration from the HARMONIOUS COLORS used on the previous page to color in this picture.

DADA

During the First World War, artists in Zürich, Switzerland, wanted to protest against the terrible things they saw happening. To do this they made what they called "anti-art," which was art that made the world appear as absurd as they thought the war was.

They picked the word "dada" at random from the dictionary to describe their movement.

Dadaists mocked traditional art by challenging what could be art. They took everyday objects and changed them in some way to create their works. For example, artist Marcel Duchamp exhibited an upside-down urinal as a sculpture, entitled "Fountain."

Dadaists believed that the choosing of the object was a creative act, and once the object was no longer used for its original function, it was art. Pieces of art that use objects in this way are called "readymades."

Get creative with these everyday objects to make your own Dadaist artwork.

Give this coat hanger arms and legs.

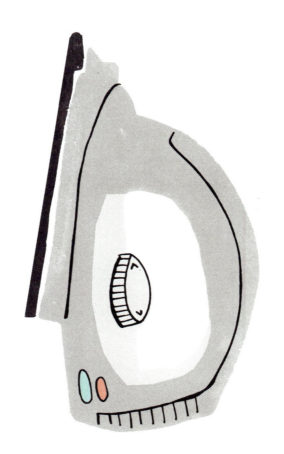

Turn this iron into an animal.

Give this cup and saucer a face.

Turn this fork into a car.

De Stijl

De Stijl, which means "the style" in Dutch, was a movement set up by artists including Piet Mondrian and Theo van Doesburg. They wanted to create a pure, simple type of art.

De Stijl was popular among many painters, architects, and sculptors.

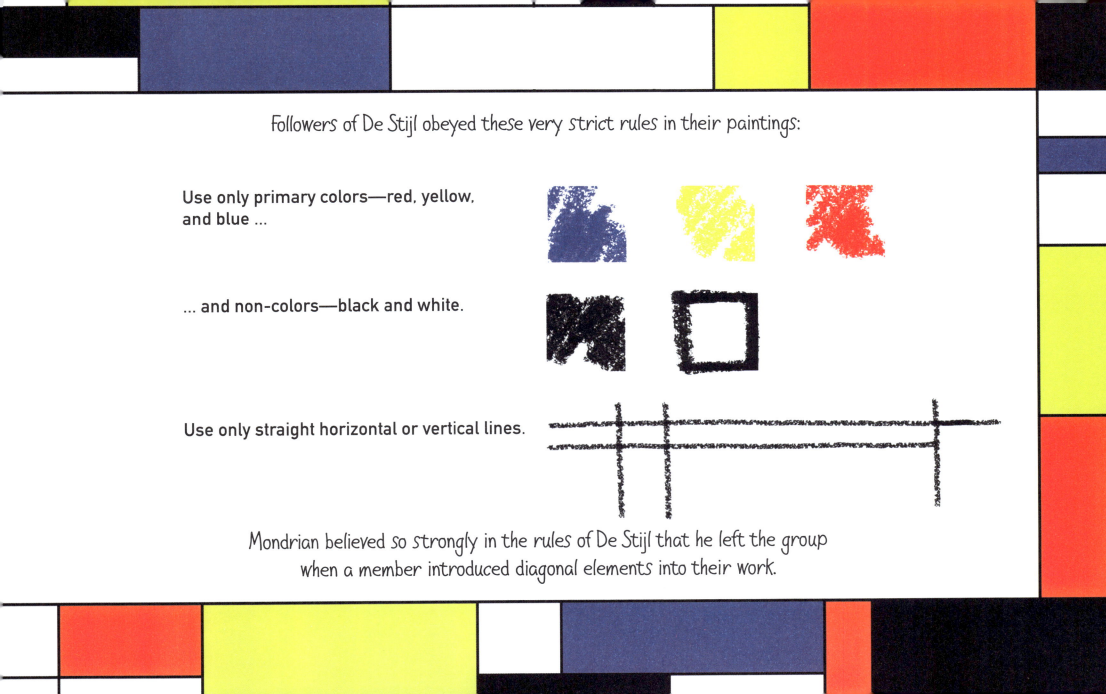

Followers of De Stijl obeyed these very strict rules in their paintings:

Use only primary colors—red, yellow, and blue ...

... and non-colors—black and white.

Use only straight horizontal or vertical lines.

Mondrian believed so strongly in the rules of De Stijl that he left the group when a member introduced diagonal elements into their work.

Finish the picture
following the
rules of De Stijl.

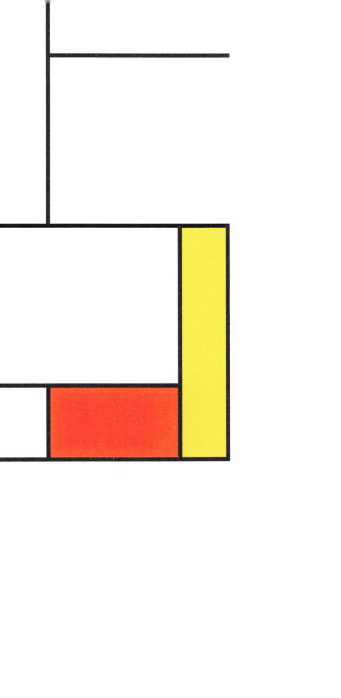

Mexican Muralism

A mural is a painting or work of art that is created directly onto a wall. Murals are a great way to tell stories and pass on messages to people who are unable to read.

In 1920, the Mexican government employed artists to paint murals on walls all over the country. They wanted the pictures to tell stories from the history of Mexico, which had been torn apart by civil war.

The government and artists, such as Diego Rivera, hoped the pictures would help bring people together and reunify the country.

Use this wall to tell your favorite story without using any words.

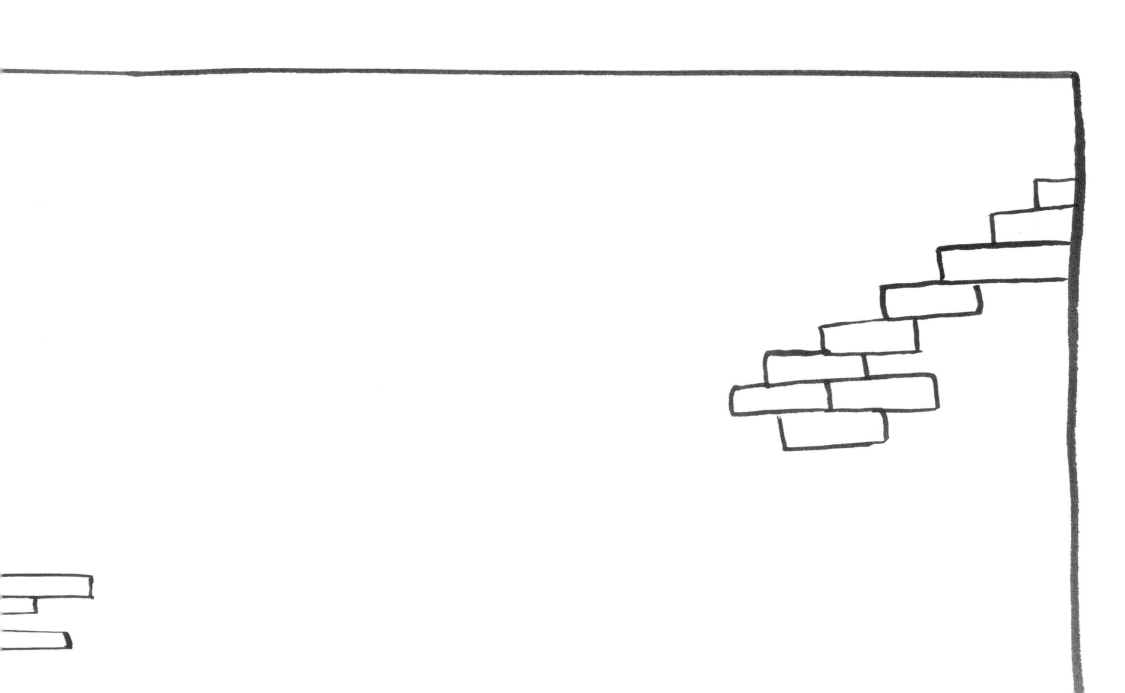

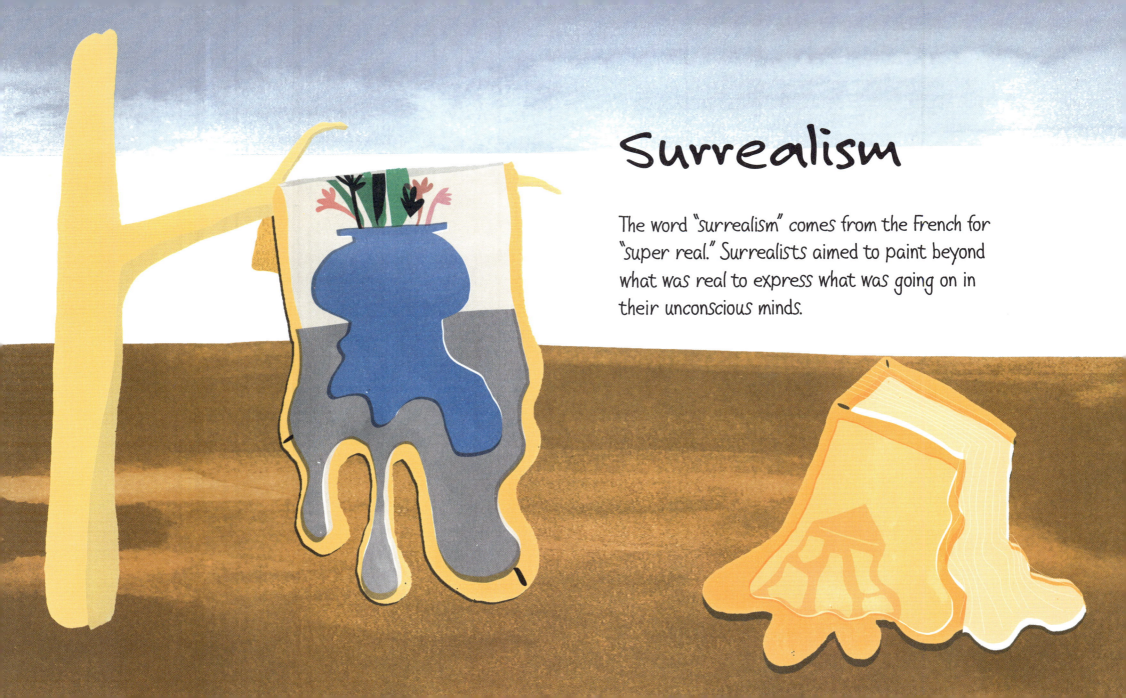

Surrealism

The word "surrealism" comes from the French for "super real." Surrealists aimed to paint beyond what was real to express what was going on in their unconscious minds.

Artist Salvador Dali expressed his unconscious mind by creating landscapes that look like something you might see in a weird dream.

Another technique Surrealist artists used was something called "automatism." With automatism, artists would purposely not think about what they were drawing or painting in order to express their subconscious mind.

Express your unconscious mind by closing your eyes and making marks on the page without thinking about what you are drawing.

Abstract Expressionism

Abstract Expressionists wanted the people looking at their work to think about what the artist was feeling as they were painting.

Nicknamed "Jack the Dripper," artist Jackson Pollock dripped, poured, and threw paint onto a canvas laid on the floor.

How would you **express** your mood right now?
Turn the page to give Abstract Expressionism a try.

THIS SCRIBBLE REPRESENTS FEELING
ANGRY.

Draw how you feel right now.

CoBrA artists wanted a style of art that felt free, and many members of the group were inspired by the work of children. They wanted their art to have the same kind of freedom children have when they paint and draw.

To do this, they made any marks they felt like making, without worrying about whether they looked like anything in real life.

The name of this style, CoBrA, comes from COpenhagen, BRussels, and Amsterdam, the initials of the founding artists' home cities.

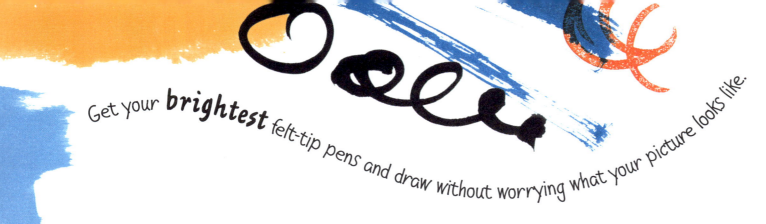

Get your **brightest** felt-tip pens and draw without worrying what your picture looks like.

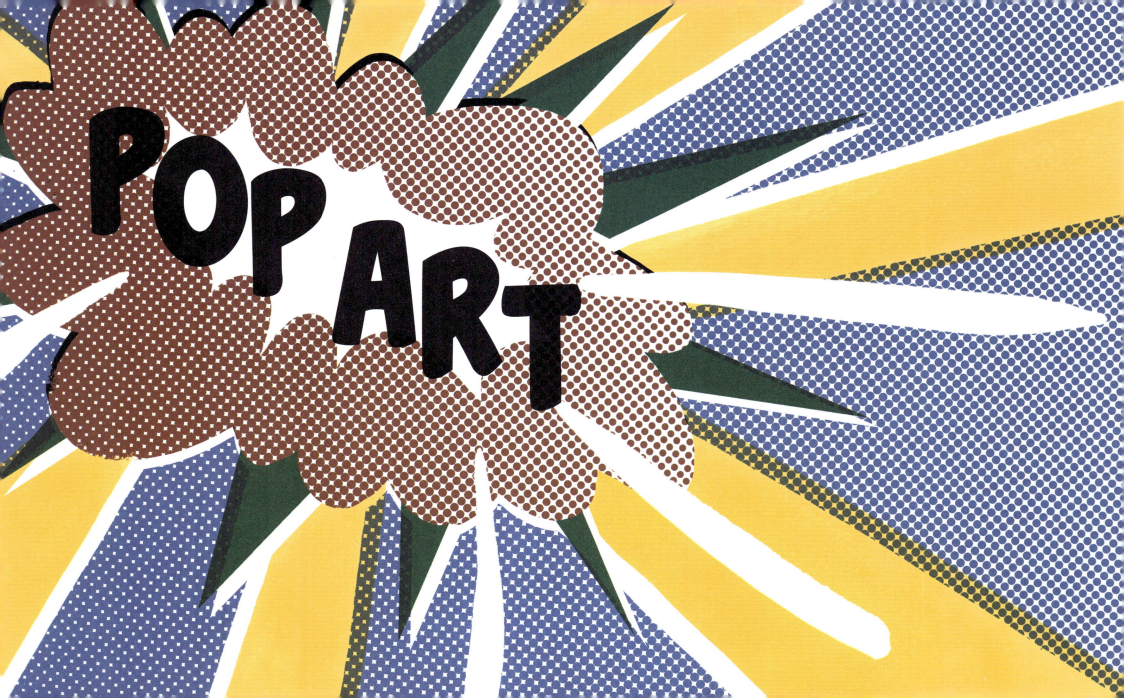

POP art was a movement that started in the 1950s, and became really POPular in the 1960s.

Pop artists wanted to create art that everyone could recognize and feel a part of. They were influenced by advertising, magazines, movies, and packaging, and used elements of all of these things in their work.

Andy Warhol was one of the most famous Pop artists. He used multiple prints of the same image to create his art, including pictures of a movie star named Marilyn Monroe and a can of tomato soup.

Roy Lichtenstein was influenced by art he saw in comics and magazines. His pictures were formed by dots of different colors and sizes, just like the dots used in printing.

MINIMALISM

The Minimalist movement was established in New York City by artists who believed art had become too much about the artists' lives and their emotions.

Minimalists wanted to create art that had no trace of the artists' personality or feelings. They used sleek geometric shapes and often used building materials to create their works.

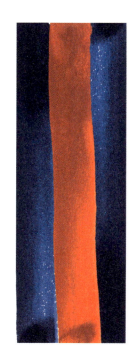

Minimalist artist Tony Smith used rolled steel to build a 6-foot cube and called his sculpture "Die."

Make your mark on Minimalist art.

Fill the page with simple shapes that say as little about you as possible. Do not color them in.

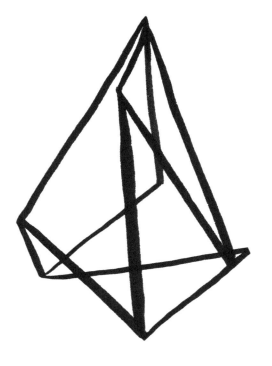

Conceptual Art

Conceptual artists believed that it is the idea behind a work that made it art, rather than the technical skill or materials used to produce it.

Artists used many art forms to express their ideas, including paint, sculpture, writing, ready-made objects, photography, and performance, sometimes in combination.

Joseph Kosuth used a ready-made clock, a photograph of a clock, and clippings from the dictionary in his work entitled "Clock (One and Five), English/Latin Version."

TELEPHONE: an instrument
for reproducing sounds at
a distance; specifically:
one in which sound is
converted into electrical
impulses for transmission
(as by wire or radio waves)

Make a list of four everyday objects below.

Draw the object here.

1.

2.

3.

4.

Now pick one object from the list to create your own piece of conceptual art.

Find a picture of the object in a magazine or newspaper and stick it here.

Describe the object here.

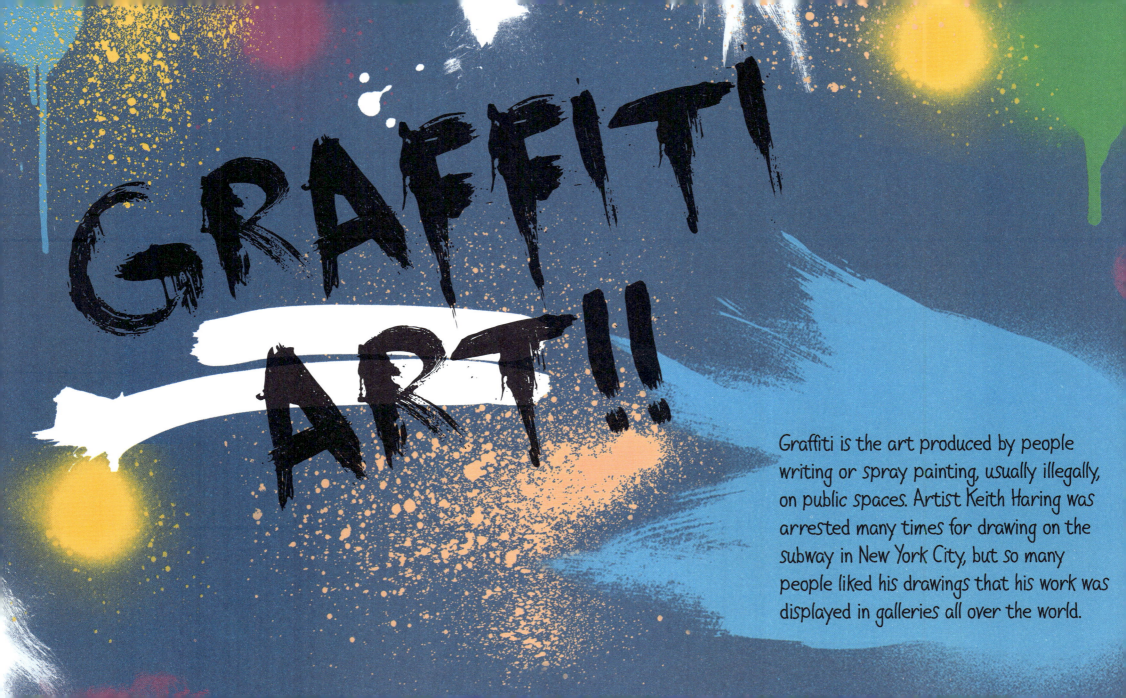

GRAFFITI ART!!

Graffiti is the art produced by people writing or spray painting, usually illegally, on public spaces. Artist Keith Haring was arrested many times for drawing on the subway in New York City, but so many people liked his drawings that his work was displayed in galleries all over the world.

There are many different types of Graffiti. **"TAGGING"** is where artists use markers to write their nicknames, or that of their crew, on public spaces. Then there are more elaborate, multicolored pictures that cover whole walls or train cars.

A British street artist known as Banksy uses stencils and paint to create his artworks. Some of his works have been carefully removed from the walls where he painted them and sold for thousands of pounds.

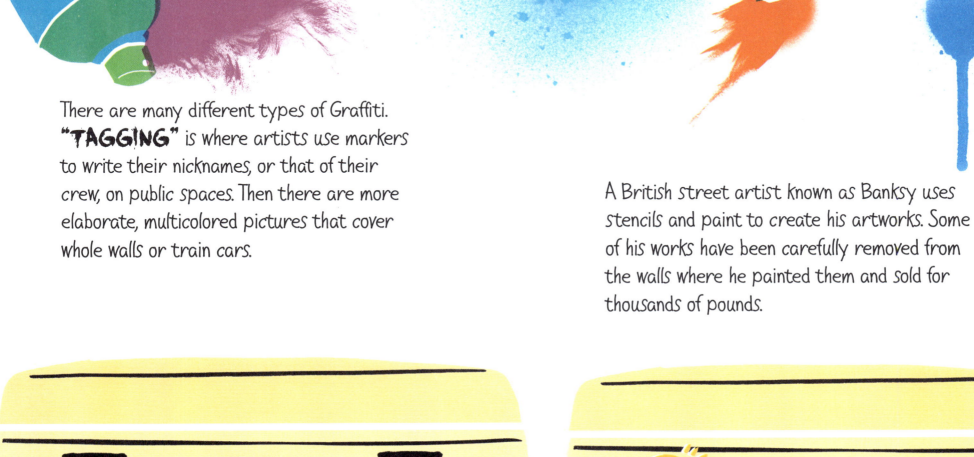

USE THIS SPACE TO COME UP WITH YOUR OWN "TAG."

Choose a nickname for yourself and experiment by writing it quickly with a broad-tipped marker pen.

The Young British Artists (YBAs) are a group of artists who displayed their work together in an exhibition called "Freeze" in 1988. The exhibition was organized by Damien Hirst, the most famous YBA. They used new and strange materials to create their art, from messy beds to whole cows preserved in enormous fishtanks.

Tracy Emin's piece "My Bed" was her own unmade bed. Emin claimed her bed was like a diary from a difficult time in her life. Some critics have said that Tracy Emin's life is a work of art in itself.

Choose three objects and make a piece of art out of them. They could be things that mean something to you, or random objects in your house. Take a picture of your piece or draw it on the next page. Don't forget to give your artwork a name.

STERLING CHILDREN'S BOOKS
New York

An Imprint of Sterling Publishing
1166 Avenue of the Americas
New York, NY 10036

First Sterling edition published in 2017.

First published in Great Britain in 2017 by Michael O'Mara Books Limited,
9 Lion Yard, Tremadoc Road, London SW4 7NQ

ISBN 978-1-4549-2563-7

Distributed in Canada by Sterling Publishing
c/o Canadian Manda Group, 664 Annette Street, Toronto, Ontario, Canada M6S 2C8

For information about custom editions, special sales, and premium and corporate purchases, please
contact Sterling Special Sales at 800-805-5489 or specialsales@sterlingpublishing.com.

Illustrations by Cindy Wilde and Felicity French, edited by Imogen Williams, designed by Zoe Bradley
Cover designed by Angie Allison

Manufactured in China

Lot #:
2 4 6 8 10 9 7 5 3 1
02/17

www.sterlingpublishing.com